JAN. 10

Test Results for Mobile Device Acquisition Tool: MOBILedit! Forensic 3.2.0.738

NCJ 228979

Kristina Rose

Acting Director, National Institute of Justice

This report was prepared for the National Institute of Justice, U.S. Department of Justice, by the Office of Law Enforcement Standards of the National Institute of Standards and Technology under Interagency Agreement 2003–IJ–R–029.

The National Institute of Justice is a component of the Office of Justice Programs, which also includes the Bureau of Justice Assistance, the Bureau of Justice Statistics, the Office of Juvenile Justice and Delinquency Prevention, and the Office for Victims of Crime.

October 2009

Test Results for Mobile Device Acquisition Tool:
MOBILedit! Forensic 3.2.0.738

**National Institute of
Standards and Technology**
U.S. Department of Commerce

Contents

Introduction

The Computer Forensics Tool Testing (CFTT) program is a joint project of the National Institute of Justice (NIJ), the research and development organization of the U.S. Department of Justice (DOJ), and the National Institute of Standards and Technology's (NIST's) Office of Law Enforcement Standards and Information Technology Laboratory. CFTT is supported by other organizations, including the Federal Bureau of Investigation, the U.S. Department of Defense Cyber Crime Center, U.S. Internal Revenue Service Criminal Investigation Division Electronic Crimes Program, and the U.S. Department of Homeland Security's Bureau of Immigration and Customs Enforcement, U.S. Customs and Border Protection and U.S. Secret Service. The objective of the CFTT program is to provide measurable assurance to practitioners, researchers, and other applicable users that the tools used in computer forensics investigations provide accurate results. Accomplishing this requires the development of specifications and test methods for computer forensics tools and subsequent testing of specific tools against those specifications.

Test results provide the information necessary for developers to improve tools, users to make informed choices, and the legal community and others to understand the tools' capabilities. This approach to testing computer forensic tools is based on well-recognized methodologies for conformance and quality testing. The specifications and test methods posted on the CFTT Web site (http://www.cftt.nist.gov/) are available for review and comment by the computer forensics community.

This document reports the results from testing MOBILedit! Forensic, version3.2.0.738, against the *Non-GSM Mobile Device and Associated Media Tool Test Assertions and Test Plan Version 1.1*, available at the CFTT Web site (www.cftt.nist.gov/mobile_devices.htm).

Test results from other software packages and the CFTT tool methodology can be found on NIJ's computer forensics tool testing Web page, http://www.ojp.usdoj.gov/nij/topics/technology/electronic-crime/cftt.htm.

Test Results for Mobile Device Data Acquisition Tool

Tool Tested: MOBILedit! Forensic
Version: 3.2.0.738
Run Environments: Windows XP Service Pack 2

Supplier: Compelson Labs

Address: COMPELSON Labs
         445 East Cypress Ave
         Los Angeles, CA 91501
WWW: http://www.mobiledit.com

1 Results Summary

Except for the following test cases: CFT–IM–01 (LG vx6100, SPH a660), CFT–IM–05 (Moto v710), CFT–IM–06 (Moto v710), CFT–IM–09 (Moto v710), CFT–IM–10 (Moto v710), and CFT–IMO–04 (Moto v710), the tested tool acquired all supported data objects completely and accurately from the selected test mobile device: Motorola v710. The exceptions are the following:

- Connectivity was not established for two supported (specified by MOBILedit! Forensic documentation) mobile devices over the supported cable interface; therefore, acquisition of device memory was not successful. Test Case: CFT–IM–01 (LG vx6100, SPH a660) – **NOTE:** The LG vx6100 must be in Brew mode – this is undocumented in the tested version – future releases will switch modes automatically for the device.
- The MEID was not reported for the Motorola v710. Test Case: CFT–IM–05 (Moto v710).
- PIM data was not reported for the Motorola v710. Test Case: CFT–IM–06 (Moto v710).
- MMS messages and corresponding attachments (audio, video, and graphic files) were not reported for the Motorola v710. Test Case: CFT–IM–09 (Moto v710).
- Stand-alone files (audio, video, and graphic files) were not reported for the Motorola v710. Test Case: CFT–IM–10 (Moto v710).
- An informative message is not returned when altering the case file data via a hex editor. Test Case: CFT–IMO–04 (Moto v710)

2 Test Case Selection

Not all test cases or test assertions are appropriate for all tools. In addition to the base test cases, each remaining test case is linked to optional tool features needed for the test case. If a given tool implements a given feature then the test cases linked to that feature are run. Tables (1a–1b) list the features available in MOBILedit! Forensic and the linked test cases. Tables (2a–2b) list the features not available in MOBILedit! Forensic. Multiple tables are necessary due to individual mobile devices providing different features. Therefore, case selection is device dependent.

Table 1a: Selected Test Cases (LG VX6100, SPH a660)

Supported Feature	Cases selected for execution
Base Cases	CFT–IM–01

Table 1b: Selected Test Cases (Moto V710)

Supported Optional Feature	Cases selected for execution
Base Cases	CFT–IM–(01–10)
Acquire mobile device internal memory and review data via supported generated report formats	CFT–IMO–01
Acquire mobile device internal memory and review reported data via the preview pane	CFT–IMO–02
Acquire mobile device internal memory and compare reported data via the preview pane and supported generated report formats	CFT–IMO–03
After a successful mobile device internal memory acquisition, alter the case file via third party means and attempt to reopen the case	CFT–IMO–04
Acquire mobile device internal memory and review generated log files	CFT–IMO–07
Acquire mobile device internal memory and review data containing foreign language characters	CFT–IMO–08

Table 2a: Omitted Test Cases (LG VX6100, SPH a660)

Test Cases not executed	Cases omitted
Base Cases	CFT–IM–(02–10)
Acquire mobile device internal memory and review data via supported generated report formats	CFT–IMO–01
Acquire mobile device internal memory and review reported data via the preview pane	CFT–IMO–02
Acquire mobile device internal memory and compare reported data via the preview pane and supported generated report formats	CFT–IMO–03
After a successful mobile device internal memory	CFT–IMO–04

Test Cases not executed	Cases omitted
acquisition, alter the case file via third party means and attempt to reopen the case	
Perform a physical acquisition and review data output for readability	CFT–IMO–05
Perform a physical acquisition and review reports for recoverable deleted data	CFT–IMO–06
Acquire mobile device internal memory and review generated log files	CFT–IMO–07
Acquire mobile device internal memory and review data containing foreign language characters	CFT–IMO–08
Acquire mobile device internal memory and review hash values for vendor supported data objects	CFT–IMO–09
Acquire mobile device internal memory and review the overall case file hash	CFT–IMO–10

Table 2b: Omitted Test Cases (Samsung SPH–a660)

Unsupported Feature / Optional Feature	Cases omitted (not executed)
Perform a physical acquisition and review data output for readability	CFT–IMO–05
Perform a physical acquisition and review reports for recoverable deleted data	CFT–IMO–06
Acquire mobile device internal memory and review hash values for vendor supported data objects	CFT–IMO–09
Acquire mobile device internal memory and review the overall case file hash	CFT–IMO–10

3 Results by Test Assertion

Tables 3a–3b summarize the test results by assertion. The column labeled **Assertions Tested** gives the text of each assertion. The column labeled **Tests** gives the number of test cases that use the given assertion. The column labeled **Anomaly** gives the section number in this report where the anomaly is discussed.

Table 3a: Assertions Tested: (LG VX6100, SPH a660)

Assertions Tested	Tests	Anomaly
A_IM–01 If a cellular forensic tool provides support for connectivity of the target device then the tool shall successfully recognize the target device via all vendor supported interfaces (e.g., cable, Bluetooth, IrDA).	1	3.1

Table 3b: Assertions Tested (Moto v710)

Assertions Tested	Tests	Anomaly
A_IM–01 If a cellular forensic tool provides support for connectivity of	9	

the target device then the tool shall successfully recognize the target device via all vendor supported interfaces (e.g., cable, Bluetooth, IrDA).		
A_IM–02 If a cellular forensic tool attempts to connect to a nonsupported device then the tool shall have the ability to identify that the device is not supported.	1	
A_IM–03 If a cellular forensic tool encounters disengagement between the device and application then the application shall notify the user that connectivity has been disrupted.	1	
A_IM–04 If a cellular forensic tool successfully completes acquisition of the target device then the tool shall have the ability to present acquired data elements in a human-readable format via either a preview pane or generated report.	7	
A_IM–05 If a cellular forensic tool successfully completes acquisition of the target device then subscriber related information shall be presented in a human-readable format without modification.	1	
A_IM–06 If a cellular forensic tool successfully completes acquisition of the target device then equipment related information shall be presented in a human-readable format without modification.	1	3.2
A_IM–07 If a cellular forensic tool successfully completes acquisition of the target device then all known address book entries shall be presented in a human-readable format without modification.	1	
A_IM–08 If a cellular forensic tool successfully completes acquisition of the target device then all known maximum length address book entries shall be presented in a human-readable format without modification.	1	
A_IM–09 If a cellular forensic tool successfully completes acquisition of the target device then all known address book entries containing special characters shall be presented in a human-readable format without modification.	1	
A_IM–10 If a cellular forensic tool successfully completes acquisition of the target device then all known address book entries containing blank names shall be presented in a human-readable format without modification.	1	
A_IM–11 If a cellular forensic tool successfully completes acquisition of the target device then all known email addresses associated with address book entries shall be presented in a human-readable format without modification.	1	
A_IM–12 If a cellular forensic tool successfully completes acquisition of the target device then all known graphics associated with address book entries shall be presented in a human-readable format without modification.	1	3.3
A_IM–13 If a cellular forensic tool successfully completes acquisition of the target device then all known datebook, calendar, note entries shall be presented in a human-readable format without modification.	1	3.3
A_IM–14 If a cellular forensic tool successfully completes acquisition of the target device then all maximum length datebook, calendar, note	1	3.3

entries shall be presented in a human readable format without modification.		
A_IM–15 If a cellular forensic tool successfully completes acquisition of the target device then all call logs (incoming/outgoing) shall be presented in a human-readable format without modification.	1	
A_IM–16 If a cellular forensic tool successfully completes acquisition of the target device then all text messages (i.e., SMS, EMS) messages shall be presented in a human-readable format without modification.	1	
A_IM–17 If a cellular forensic tool successfully completes acquisition of the target device then all MMS messages and associated audio shall be presented properly without modification.	1	3.4
A_IM–18 If a cellular forensic tool successfully completes acquisition of the target device then all MMS messages and associated images shall be presented properly without modification.	1	3.4
A_IM–19 If a cellular forensic tool successfully completes acquisition of the target device then all MMS messages and associated video shall be presented properly without modification.	1	3.4
A_IM–20 If a cellular forensic tool successfully completes acquisition of the target device then all stand-alone audio files shall be playable via either an internal application or suggested third-party application without modification.	1	3.5
A_IM–21 If a cellular forensic tool successfully completes acquisition of the target device then all stand-alone image files shall be viewable via either an internal application or suggested third-party application without modification.	1	3.5
A_IM–22 If a cellular forensic tool successfully completes acquisition of the target device then all stand-alone video files shall be viewable via either an internal application or suggested third-party application without modification.	1	3.5
A_IMO–23 If a cellular forensic tool successfully completes acquisition of the target device then the tool shall present the acquired data without modification via supported generated report formats.	3	
A_IMO–24 If a cellular forensic tool successfully completes acquisition of the target device then the tool shall present the acquired data without modification in a preview-pane view.	3	
A_IMO–25 If a cellular forensic tool provides a preview-pane view and a generated report of the acquired data then the reports shall maintain consistency of all reported data elements.	1	
A_IMO–26 If modification is attempted to the case file or individual data elements via third-party means then the tool shall provide protection mechanisms disallowing or reporting data modification.	1	3.6
A_IMO–36 If the cellular forensic tool supports log creation then the application should present the log files consistent with the application documentation (e.g., outlining the acquisition process).	1	
A_IMO–37 If the cellular forensic tool supports proper display of	1	

foreign language character sets then the application should present address book entries containing foreign language characters in their native format without modification.		
A_IMO–38 If the cellular forensic tool supports proper display of foreign language character sets then the application should present text messages containing foreign language characters in their native format without modification.	1	

Tables 4a–4b list the assertions that were not tested, usually due to the tool not supporting an optional feature.

Table 4a: Assertions Not Tested (LG VX6100, SPH a660)

Assertions not Tested
A_IM–02 If a cellular forensic tool attempts to connect to a nonsupported device then the tool shall have the ability to identify that the device is not supported.
A_IM–03 If a cellular forensic tool encounters disengagement between the device and application then the application shall notify the user that connectivity has been disrupted.
A_IM–04 If a cellular forensic tool successfully completes acquisition of the target device then the tool shall have the ability to present acquired data elements in a human-readable format via either a preview pane or generated report.
A_IM–05 If a cellular forensic tool successfully completes acquisition of the target device then subscriber related information shall be presented in a human-readable format without modification.
A_IM–06 If a cellular forensic tool successfully completes acquisition of the target device then equipment related information shall be presented in a human-readable format without modification.
A_IM–07 If a cellular forensic tool successfully completes acquisition of the target device then all known address book entries shall be presented in a human-readable format without modification.
A_IM–08 If a cellular forensic tool successfully completes acquisition of the target device then all known maximum length address book entries shall be presented in a human-readable format without modification.
A_IM–09 If a cellular forensic tool successfully completes acquisition of the target device then all known address book entries containing special characters shall be presented in a human-readable format without modification.
A_IM–10 If a cellular forensic tool successfully completes acquisition of the target device then all known address book entries containing blank names shall be presented in a human-readable format without modification.
A_IM–11 If a cellular forensic tool successfully completes acquisition of the target device then all known email addresses associated with address book entries shall be presented in a human-readable format without modification.
A_IM–12 If a cellular forensic tool successfully completes acquisition of the target device then all known graphics associated with address book entries shall be presented in a human-readable format without modification.
A_IM–13 If a cellular forensic tool successfully completes acquisition of the target device then all known datebook, calendar, note entries shall be presented in a human-readable

format without modification.
A_IM–14 If a cellular forensic tool successfully completes acquisition of the target device then all maximum length datebook, calendar, note entries shall be presented in a human readable format without modification.
A_IM–15 If a cellular forensic tool successfully completes acquisition of the target device then all call logs (incoming/outgoing) shall be presented in a human-readable format without modification.
A_IM–16 If a cellular forensic tool successfully completes acquisition of the target device then all text messages (i.e., SMS, EMS) shall be presented in a human-readable format without modification.
A_IM–17 If a cellular forensic tool successfully completes acquisition of the target device then all MMS messages and associated audio shall be presented properly without modification.
A_IM–18 If a cellular forensic tool successfully completes acquisition of the target device then all MMS messages and associated images shall be presented properly without modification.
A_IM–19 If a cellular forensic tool successfully completes acquisition of the target device then all MMS messages and associated video shall be presented properly without modification.
A_IM–20 If a cellular forensic tool successfully completes acquisition of the target device then all stand-alone audio files shall be playable via either an internal application or suggested third-party application without modification.
A_IM–21 If a cellular forensic tool successfully completes acquisition of the target device then all stand-alone image files shall be viewable via either an internal application or suggested third-party application without modification.
A_IM–22 If a cellular forensic tool successfully completes acquisition of the target device then all stand-alone video files shall be viewable via either an internal application or suggested third-party application without modification.
A_IMO–23 If a cellular forensic tool successfully completes acquisition of the target device then the tool shall present the acquired data without modification via supported generated report formats.
A_IMO–24 If a cellular forensic tool successfully completes acquisition of the target device then the tool shall present the acquired data without modification in a preview-pane view.
A_IMO–25 If a cellular forensic tool provides a preview-pane view and a generated report of the acquired data then the reports shall maintain consistency of all reported data elements.
A_IMO–26 If modification is attempted to the case file or individual data elements via third-party means then the tool shall provide protection mechanisms disallowing or reporting data modification.
A_IMO–27 If the cellular forensic tool supports a physical acquisition of the target device then the tool shall successfully complete the acquisition and present the data in a human-readable format.
A_IMO–28 If the cellular forensic tool supports a physical acquisition of address book entries present on the target device then the tool shall report recoverable deleted entries or

data remnants in a human-readable format.

A_IMO–29 If the cellular forensic tool supports a physical acquisition of calendar, tasks, or notes present on the target device then the tool shall report recoverable deleted calendar, tasks, or note entries or data remnants in a human-readable format.
A_IMO–30 If the cellular forensic tool supports a physical acquisition of call logs present on the target device then the tool shall report recoverable deleted call log data or data remnants in a human-readable format.
A_IMO–31 If the cellular forensic tool supports a physical acquisition of SMS messages present on the target device then the tool shall report recoverable deleted SMS messages or SMS message data remnants in a human-readable format.
A_IMO–32 If the cellular forensic tool supports a physical acquisition of EMS messages present on the target device then the tool shall report recoverable deleted EMS messages or EMS message data remnants in a human-readable format.
A_IMO–33 If the cellular forensic tool supports a physical acquisition of audio files present on the target device then the tool shall report recoverable deleted audio data or audio file data remnants in a human-readable format.
A_IMO–34 If the cellular forensic tool supports a physical acquisition of graphic files present on the target device then the tool shall report recoverable deleted graphic file data or graphic file data remnants in a human-readable format.
A_IMO–35 If the cellular forensic tool supports a physical acquisition of video files present on the target device then the tool shall report recoverable deleted video file data or video file data remnants in a human-readable format.
A_IMO–36 If the cellular forensic tool supports log creation then the application should present the log files consistent with the application documentation (e.g., outlining the acquisition process).
A_IMO–37 If the cellular forensic tool supports proper display of foreign language character sets then the application should present address book entries containing foreign language characters in their native format without modification.
A_IMO–38 If the cellular forensic tool supports proper display of foreign language character sets then the application should present text messages containing foreign language characters in their native format without modification.
A_IMO–39 If the cellular forensic tool supports hashing for individual data objects then the tool shall present the user with a hash value for each supported data object.
A_IMO–40 If the cellular forensic tool supports hashing the overall case file then the tool shall present the user with one hash value representing the entire case data.

Table 4b: Assertions Not Tested (Motorola V710)

Assertions not Tested
A_IMO–27 If the cellular forensic tool supports a physical acquisition of the target device then the tool shall successfully complete the acquisition and present the data in a human-readable format.
A_IMO–28 If the cellular forensic tool supports a physical acquisition of address book entries present on the target device then the tool shall report recoverable deleted entries or data remnants in a human-readable format.
A_IMO–29 If the cellular forensic tool supports a physical acquisition of calendar, tasks,

or notes present on the target device then the tool shall report recoverable deleted calendar, tasks, or note entries or data remnants in a human-readable format.
A_IMO–30 If the cellular forensic tool supports a physical acquisition of call logs present on the target device then the tool shall report recoverable deleted call log data or data remnants in a human-readable format.
A_IMO–31 If the cellular forensic tool supports a physical acquisition of SMS messages present on the target device then the tool shall report recoverable deleted SMS messages or SMS message data remnants in a human-readable format.
A_IMO–32 If the cellular forensic tool supports a physical acquisition of EMS messages present on the target device then the tool shall report recoverable deleted EMS messages or EMS message data remnants in a human-readable format.
A_IMO–33 If the cellular forensic tool supports a physical acquisition of audio files present on the target device then the tool shall report recoverable deleted audio data or audio file data remnants in a human-readable format.
A_IMO–34 If the cellular forensic tool supports a physical acquisition of graphic files present on the target device then the tool shall report recoverable deleted graphic file data or graphic file data remnants in a human-readable format.
A_IMO–35 If the cellular forensic tool supports a physical acquisition of video files present on the target device then the tool shall report recoverable deleted video file data or video file data remnants in a human-readable format.
A_IMO–39 If the cellular forensic tool supports hashing for individual data objects then the tool shall present the user with a hash value for each supported data object.
A_IMO–40 If the cellular forensic tool supports hashing the overall case file then the tool shall present the user with one hash value representing the entire case data.

3.1 Connectivity

Mobiledit was unable to successfully connect to the LG vx6100 and the Samsung SPH a660. The LG vx6100 is displayed under Ports and the Samsung SPH a660 is displayed under Modems under Windows XP's Device Manager. Mobiledit's Forensic Settings lists the ports consistent with Windows XP's device manager as an option for device acquisition.

When attempting to connect to the LG vx6100 and the Samsung SPH a660 via Mobiledit's forensic wizard the proper port is queried but the connectivity to the device is not established.

Note: The LG vx6100 must be in Brew mode – this is undocumented in the tested version – future releases will switch modes automatically for the device.

Connection of various devices in MOBILEdit! (ME) architecture is done via "mobiledit drivers". Application drivers are registered in "driver manager". If detection is started on some port, driver manager periodically attempts connectivity via each registered driver. The connectivity issue with the Samsung A660 is the following:
- ME uses driver CDMA for it.
- Samsung2 driver is registered in system before CDMA driver.
- Samsung2 has detection routine which handles all Samsung phones except some "exceptions" problem is that A660 was no properly handled as exception so phone was handled as generic GSM Samsung. A quick fix is to disable Samsung2 driver by removing it.

3.2 Acquisition of Equipment Related Data

The MEID was reported as a blank entry for the Motorola v710.

3.3 Acquisition of PIM Data

The following Personal Information Management (PIM) data was not reported for the Motorola v710: graphics files associated with address book entries and calendar / Notes entries.

3.4 Acquisition of MMS Messages / Data

MMS messages and related data (i.e., audio, video, and graphic files) were not reported for the Motorola v710.

3.5 Acquisition of Stand-alone Data Files

Stand-alone data files (i.e., audio, video, and graphic files) were not reported for the Motorola v710.

3.6 Data Integrity

No warning messages are provided to the user when a case file has been modified with a hex editor in a fashion that results in inconsistent case file data compared to the original case file.

The modified case file is simply removed from the GUI as a selectable case.

4   Testing Environment

The tests were run in the NIST CFTT lab. This section describes the test computers available for testing.

One test computer was used.

Morrisy has the following configuration:

Intel® D975XBX2 Motherboard
BIOS Version BX97520J.86A.2674.2007.0315.1546
Intel® Core™2 Duo CPU 6700 @ 2.66Ghz
3.25 GB RAM
1.44 MB floppy drive
LITE-ON CD H LH52N1P
LITE-ON DVDRW LH–20A1P
2 slots for removable SATA hard disk drive
8 USB 2.0 slots
2 IEEE 1394 ports
3 IEEE 1394 ports (mini)

5 Test Results

The main item of interest for interpreting the test results is determining the conformance of the device with the test assertions. Conformance with each assertion tested by a given test case is evaluated by examining **Log File Highlights** box of the test report summary.

5.1 Test Results Report Key

A summary of the actual test results is presented in this report. The following table presents a description of each section of the test report summary.

Table 5 Test Results Report Key

Heading	Description
First Line:	Test case ID, name, and version of tool tested.
Case Summary:	Test case summary from *Non-GSM Mobile Tool Test Assertions and Test Plan Version 1.1*.
Assertions:	The test assertions applicable to the test case, selected from *Non-GSM Mobile Device Tool Test Assertions and Test Plan Version 1.1*.
Tester Name:	Name or initials of person executing test procedure.
Test Host:	Host computer executing the test.
Test Date:	Time and date that test was started.
Device:	Source mobile device, media (i.e., SIM).
Source Setup:	Outline of data object types populated on the device.
Log Highlights:	Information extracted from various log files to illustrate conformance or nonconformance to the test assertions.
Results:	Expected and actual results for each assertion tested.
Analysis:	Whether or not the expected results were achieved.

5.2 Test Details

5.2.1 CFT-IM-01 (LG VX6100)

Test Case CFT-IM-01 MOBILedit 3.2.0.738	
Case Summary:	CFT-IM-01 Acquire mobile device internal memory over supported interfaces (e.g., cable, Bluetooth, IrDA).
Assertions:	A_IM-01 If a cellular forensic tool provides support for connectivity of the target device then the tool shall successfully recognize the target device via all vendor supported interfaces (e.g., cable, Bluetooth, IrDA).
Tester Name:	rpa
Test Host:	Morrisy
Test Date:	Mon Aug 24 09:28:41 EDT 2009
Device:	LG_vx6100
Source Setup:	OS: WIN XP Interface: cable

DATA OBJECTS	DATA ELEMENTS
Address Book Entries	
	Maximum Length
	Regular Length, email, picture
	Special Character
	Blank Name
	Regular Length, Deleted email - deleted picture
	Deleted Entry
	Foreign Entry
PIM Data	
	Maximum Length
	Regular Length
	Deleted Entry
	Special Character
Call Logs	
	Missed
	Missed - Deleted
	Incoming
	Incoming - Deleted
	Outgoing
	Outgoing - Deleted
Text Messages	
	Incoming SMS - Read
	Incoming SMS - Unread
	Incoming SMS - Deleted
	Outgoing SMS
	Outgoing SMS - Deleted
	Incoming EMS - Read
	Incoming EMS - Unread
	Incoming Foreign EMS - Read
	Incoming EMS - Deleted
	Outgoing EMS
	Outgoing EMS - Deleted
MMS Messages	
	Incoming Audio
	Incoming Image
	Incoming Video
	Outgoing Audio
	Outgoing Image
	Outgoing Video
Stand-alone data files	
	Audio
	Audio - Deleted
	Image
	Image - Deleted
	Video
	Video - Deleted

Test Case CFT-IM-01 MOBILedit 3.2.0.738	
Log Highlights:	Created By MOBILedit! Version 3.2.0.738 Acquisition started: Mon Aug 24 09:28:41 EDT 2009 Acquisition finished: Mon Aug 24 09:31:26 EDT 2009 Device Connectivity was not established via supported interface **Notes:** Mobiledit was unable to successfully connect to the LG vx6100. The device is displayed under Ports by Windows XP's Device Manager. Additionally, Mobiledit's Forensic Settings list the port consistent with Windows XP's device manager as an option for device acquisition. When attempting to connect to the LG vx6100 via Mobiledit's forensic wizard the proper port is queried but the connectivity to the device is not established.
Results:	<table><tr><th>Assertion & Expected Result</th><th>Actual Result</th></tr><tr><td>A IM-01 Device connectivity via supported interfaces.</td><td>Not as expected</td></tr></table>
Analysis:	Expected results NOT achieved

5.2.2 CFT-IM-01 (Moto v710)

Test Case CFT-IM-01 MOBILedit 3.2.0.738	
Case Summary:	CFT-IM-01 Acquire mobile device internal memory over supported interfaces (e.g., cable, Bluetooth, IrDA).
Assertions:	A_IM-01 If a cellular forensic tool provides support for connectivity of the target device then the tool shall successfully recognize the target device via all vendor supported interfaces (e.g., cable, Bluetooth, IrDA).
Tester Name:	rpa
Test Host:	Morrisy
Test Date:	Tue Aug 25 08:24:59 EDT 2009
Device:	Motorola v710
Source Setup:	OS: WIN XP Interface: cable

DATA OBJECTS	DATA ELEMENTS
Address Book Entries	
	Maximum Length
	Regular Length, email, picture
	Special Character
	Blank Name
	Regular Length, Deleted email - deleted picture
	Deleted Entry
	Foreign Entry
PIM Data	
	Maximum Length
	Regular Length
	Deleted Entry
	Special Character
Call Logs	
	Missed
	Missed - Deleted
	Incoming
	Incoming - Deleted
	Outgoing
	Outgoing - Deleted
Text Messages	
	Incoming SMS - Read
	Incoming SMS - Unread
	Incoming SMS - Deleted
	Outgoing SMS
	Outgoing SMS - Deleted
	Incoming EMS - Read
	Incoming EMS - Unread
	Incoming Foreign EMS - Read
	Incoming EMS - Deleted
	Outgoing EMS
	Outgoing EMS - Deleted
MMS Messages	
	Incoming Audio
	Incoming Image
	Incoming Video
	Outgoing Audio
	Outgoing Image
	Outgoing Video
Stand-alone data files	
	Audio
	Audio - Deleted
	Image
	Image - Deleted
	Video
	Video - Deleted

Log	Created By MOBILedit! Version 3.2.0.738

```
Test Case CFT-IM-01 MOBILedit 3.2.0.738
```

Highlights:	Acquisition started: Tue Aug 25 08:24:59 EDT 2009 Acquisition finished: Tue Aug 25 08:34:35 EDT 2009 Device connectivity was established via supported interface
Results:	

Assertion & Expected Result	Actual Result
A IM-01 Device connectivity via supported interfaces.	as expected

Analysis:	Expected results achieved

5.2.3 CFT-IM-02 (Moto v710)

Test Case CFT-IM-02 MOBILedit 3.2.0.738	
Case Summary:	CFT-IM-02 Attempt internal memory acquisition of a non-supported mobile device.
Assertions:	A_IM-02 If a cellular forensic tool attempts to connect to a non-supported device then the tool shall have the ability to identify that the device is not supported.
Tester Name:	rpa
Test Host:	Morrisy
Test Date:	Tue Aug 25 08:36:36 EDT 2009
Device:	non supported device
Source Setup:	OS: WIN XP Interface: cable

DATA OBJECTS	DATA ELEMENTS
Address Book Entries	
	Maximum Length
	Regular Length, email, picture
	Special Character
	Blank Name
	Regular Length, Deleted email - deleted picture
	Deleted Entry
	Foreign Entry
PIM Data	
	Maximum Length
	Regular Length
	Deleted Entry
	Special Character
Call Logs	
	Missed
	Missed - Deleted
	Incoming
	Incoming - Deleted
	Outgoing
	Outgoing - Deleted
Text Messages	
	Incoming SMS - Read
	Incoming SMS - Unread
	Incoming SMS - Deleted
	Outgoing SMS
	Outgoing SMS - Deleted
	Incoming EMS - Read
	Incoming EMS - Unread
	Incoming Foreign EMS - Read
	Incoming EMS - Deleted
	Outgoing EMS
	Outgoing EMS - Deleted
MMS Messages	
	Incoming Audio
	Incoming Image
	Incoming Video
	Outgoing Audio
	Outgoing Image
	Outgoing Video
Stand-alone data files	
	Audio
	Audio - Deleted
	Image
	Image - Deleted
	Video
	Video - Deleted

Log	Created By MOBILedit! Version 3.2.0.738

Test Case CFT-IM-02 MOBILedit 3.2.0.738	
Highlights:	Acquisition started: Tue Aug 25 08:36:36 EDT 2009 Acquisition finished: Tue Aug 25 08:49:57 EDT 2009 Identification of non-supported devices was successful
Results:	

Assertion & Expected Result	Actual Result
A IM-02 Identification of non-supported devices.	as expected

Analysis:	Expected results achieved

5.2.4 CFT-IM-03 (Moto v710)

Test Case CFT-IM-03 MOBILedit 3.2.0.738	
Case Summary:	CFT-IM-03 Begin mobile device internal memory acquisition and interrupt connectivity by interface disengagement.
Assertions:	A_IM-01 If a cellular forensic tool provides support for connectivity of the target device then the tool shall successfully recognize the target device via all vendor supported interfaces (e.g., cable, Bluetooth, IrDA). A_IM-03 If a cellular forensic tool encounters disengagement between the device and application then the application shall notify the user that connectivity has been disrupted.
Tester Name:	rpa
Test Host:	Morrisy
Test Date:	Tue Aug 25 08:50:18 EDT 2009
Device:	Motorola v710
Source Setup:	OS: WIN XP Interface: cable

DATA OBJECTS	DATA ELEMENTS
Address Book Entries	
	Maximum Length
	Regular Length, email, picture
	Special Character
	Blank Name
	Regular Length, Deleted email - deleted picture
	Deleted Entry
	Foreign Entry
PIM Data	
	Maximum Length
	Regular Length
	Deleted Entry
	Special Character
Call Logs	
	Missed
	Missed - Deleted
	Incoming
	Incoming - Deleted
	Outgoing
	Outgoing - Deleted
Text Messages	
	Incoming SMS - Read
	Incoming SMS - Unread
	Incoming SMS - Deleted
	Outgoing SMS
	Outgoing SMS - Deleted
	Incoming EMS - Read
	Incoming EMS - Unread
	Incoming Foreign EMS - Read
	Incoming EMS - Deleted
	Outgoing EMS
	Outgoing EMS - Deleted
MMS Messages	
	Incoming Audio
	Incoming Image
	Incoming Video
	Outgoing Audio
	Outgoing Image
	Outgoing Video
Stand-alone data files	
	Audio
	Audio - Deleted
	Image
	Image - Deleted
	Video
	Video - Deleted

Test Case CFT-IM-03 MOBILedit 3.2.0.738	
Log Highlights:	Created By MOBILedit! Version 3.2.0.738 Acquisition started: Tue Aug 25 08:50:18 EDT 2009 Acquisition finished: Tue Aug 25 08:54:17 EDT 2009 Device connectivity was established via supported interface Device acquisition disruption notification was successful
Results:	

Assertion & Expected Result	Actual Result
A IM-01 Device connectivity via supported interfaces.	as expected
A_IM-03 Notification of device acquisition disruption.	as expected

Analysis:	Expected results achieved

5.2.5 CFT-IM-04 (Moto v710)

Test Case CFT-IM-04 MOBILedit 3.2.0.738	
Case Summary:	CFT-IM-04 Acquire mobile device internal memory and review reported data via the preview-pane or generated reports for readability.
Assertions:	A_IM-01 If a cellular forensic tool provides support for connectivity of the target device then the tool shall successfully recognize the target device via all vendor supported interfaces (e.g., cable, Bluetooth, IrDA). A_IM-04 If a cellular forensic tool successfully completes acquisition of the target device then the tool shall have the ability to present acquired data elements in a human-readable format via either a preview-pane or generated report.
Tester Name:	rpa
Test Host:	Morrisy
Test Date:	Tue Aug 25 09:01:27 EDT 2009
Device:	Motorola v710
Source Setup:	OS: WIN XP Interface: cable

DATA OBJECTS	DATA ELEMENTS
Address Book Entries	
	Maximum Length
	Regular Length, email, picture
	Special Character
	Blank Name
	Regular Length, Deleted email - deleted picture
	Deleted Entry
	Foreign Entry
PIM Data	
	Maximum Length
	Regular Length
	Deleted Entry
	Special Character
Call Logs	
	Missed
	Missed - Deleted
	Incoming
	Incoming - Deleted
	Outgoing
	Outgoing - Deleted
Text Messages	
	Incoming SMS - Read
	Incoming SMS - Unread
	Incoming SMS - Deleted
	Outgoing SMS
	Outgoing SMS - Deleted
	Incoming EMS - Read
	Incoming EMS - Unread
	Incoming Foreign EMS - Read
	Incoming EMS - Deleted
	Outgoing EMS
	Outgoing EMS - Deleted
MMS Messages	
	Incoming Audio
	Incoming Image
	Incoming Video
	Outgoing Audio
	Outgoing Image
	Outgoing Video
Stand-alone data files	
	Audio
	Audio - Deleted
	Image
	Image - Deleted
	Video

Test Case CFT-IM-04 MOBILedit 3.2.0.738	
	Video - Deleted
Log Highlights:	Created By MOBILedit! Version 3.2.0.738 Acquisition started: Tue Aug 25 09:01:27 EDT 2009 Acquisition finished: Tue Aug 25 09:07:10 EDT 2009 Device connectivity was established via supported interface Readability and completeness of acquired data was successful
Results:	

Assertion & Expected Result	Actual Result
A_IM-01 Device connectivity via supported interfaces.	as expected
A_IM-04 Readability and completeness of acquired data via supported reports.	as expected

Analysis:	Expected results achieved

5.2.6 CFT-IM-05 (Moto v710)

Test Case CFT-IM-05 MOBILedit 3.2.0.738	
Case Summary:	CFT-IM-05 Acquire mobile device internal memory and review reported subscriber and equipment related information (i.e., MEID, MSISDN).
Assertions:	A_IM-01 If a cellular forensic tool provides support for connectivity of the target device then the tool shall successfully recognize the target device via all vendor supported interfaces (e.g., cable, Bluetooth, IrDA). A_IM-04 If a cellular forensic tool successfully completes acquisition of the target device then the tool shall have the ability to present acquired data elements in a human-readable format via either a preview-pane or generated report. A_IM-05 If a cellular forensic tool successfully completes acquisition of the target device then subscriber related information shall be presented in a human-readable format without modification. A_IM-06 If a cellular forensic tool successfully completes acquisition of the target device then equipment related information shall be presented in a human-readable format without modification.
Tester Name:	rpa
Test Host:	Morrisy
Test Date:	Tue Aug 25 09:07:35 EDT 2009
Device:	Motorola v710
Source Setup:	OS: WIN XP Interface: cable

DATA OBJECTS	DATA ELEMENTS
Address Book Entries	
	Maximum Length
	Regular Length, email, picture
	Special Character
	Blank Name
	Regular Length, Deleted email - deleted picture
	Deleted Entry
	Foreign Entry
PIM Data	
	Maximum Length
	Regular Length
	Deleted Entry
	Special Character
Call Logs	
	Missed
	Missed - Deleted
	Incoming
	Incoming - Deleted
	Outgoing
	Outgoing - Deleted
Text Messages	
	Incoming SMS - Read
	Incoming SMS - Unread
	Incoming SMS - Deleted
	Outgoing SMS
	Outgoing SMS - Deleted
	Incoming EMS - Read
	Incoming EMS - Unread
	Incoming Foreign EMS - Read
	Incoming EMS - Deleted
	Outgoing EMS
	Outgoing EMS - Deleted
MMS Messages	
	Incoming Audio
	Incoming Image
	Incoming Video
	Outgoing Audio
	Outgoing Image
	Outgoing Video

Test Case CFT-IM-05 MOBILedit 3.2.0.738		
	Stand-alone data files	
		Audio
		Audio - Deleted
		Image
		Image - Deleted
		Video
		Video - Deleted

Log Highlights:	Created By MOBILedit! Version 3.2.0.738 Acquisition started: Tue Aug 25 09:07:35 EDT 2009 Acquisition finished: Tue Aug 25 09:19:25 EDT 2009 Device connectivity was established via supported interface Readability and completeness of acquired data was successful Subscriber and Equipment related data (i.e., MSISDN, MEID) were partially acquired **Notes:** The ESN was not reported.

Results:

Assertion & Expected Result	Actual Result
A_IM-01 Device connectivity via supported interfaces.	as expected
A_IM-04 Readability and completeness of acquired data via supported reports.	as expected
A_IM-05 Acquisition of MSISDN.	as expected
A_IM-06 Acquisition of MEID.	Not as expected

Analysis:	Partial results achieved

5.2.7 CFT-IM-06 (Moto v710)

Test Case CFT-IM-06 MOBILedit 3.2.0.738	
Case Summary:	CFT-IM-06 Acquire mobile device internal memory and review reported PIM related data.
Assertions:	A_IM-01 If a cellular forensic tool provides support for connectivity of the target device then the tool shall successfully recognize the target device via all vendor supported interfaces (e.g., cable, Bluetooth, IrDA). A_IM-04 If a cellular forensic tool successfully completes acquisition of the target device then the tool shall have the ability to present acquired data elements in a human-readable format via either a preview-pane or generated report. A_IM-07 If a cellular forensic tool successfully completes acquisition of the target device then all known address book entries shall be presented in a human-readable format without modification. A_IM-08 If a cellular forensic tool successfully completes acquisition of the target device then all known maximum length address book entries shall be presented in a human-readable format without modification. A_IM-09 If a cellular forensic tool successfully completes acquisition of the target device then all known address book entries containing special characters shall be presented in a human-readable format without modification. A_IM-10 If a cellular forensic tool successfully completes acquisition of the target device then all known address book entries containing blank names shall be presented in a human-readable format without modification. A_IM-11 If a cellular forensic tool successfully completes acquisition of the target device then all known email addresses associated with address book entries shall be presented in a human-readable format without modification. A_IM-12 If a cellular forensic tool successfully completes acquisition of the target device then all known graphics associated with address book entries shall be presented in a human-readable format without modification. A_IM-13 If a cellular forensic tool successfully completes acquisition of the target device then all known datebook, calendar, note entries shall be presented in a human-readable format without modification. A_IM-14 If a cellular forensic tool successfully completes acquisition of the target device then all maximum length datebook, calendar, note entries shall be presented in a human readable format without modification.
Tester Name:	rpa
Test Host:	Morrisy
Test Date:	Tue Aug 25 09:23:30 EDT 2009
Device:	Motorola v710
Source Setup:	OS: WIN XP Interface: cable

DATA OBJECTS	DATA ELEMENTS
Address Book Entries	
	Maximum Length
	Regular Length, email, picture
	Special Character
	Blank Name
	Regular Length, Deleted email - deleted picture
	Deleted Entry
	Foreign Entry
PIM Data	
	Maximum Length
	Regular Length
	Deleted Entry
	Special Character
Call Logs	
	Missed
	Missed - Deleted
	Incoming
	Incoming - Deleted
	Outgoing
	Outgoing - Deleted

	Text Messages		
		Incoming SMS - Read	
		Incoming SMS - Unread	
		Incoming SMS - Deleted	
		Outgoing SMS	
		Outgoing SMS - Deleted	
		Incoming EMS - Read	
		Incoming EMS - Unread	
		Incoming Foreign EMS - Read	
		Incoming EMS - Deleted	
		Outgoing EMS	
		Outgoing EMS - Deleted	
	MMS Messages		
		Incoming Audio	
		Incoming Image	
		Incoming Video	
		Outgoing Audio	
		Outgoing Image	
		Outgoing Video	
	Stand-alone data files		
		Audio	
		Audio - Deleted	
		Image	
		Image - Deleted	
		Video	
		Video - Deleted	

Log Highlights:	Created By MOBILedit! Version 3.2.0.738 Acquisition started: Tue Aug 25 09:23:30 EDT 2009 Acquisition finished: Tue Aug 25 09:25:54 EDT 2009 Device connectivity was established via supported interface Readability and completeness of acquired data was successful All address book entries were successfully acquired Basic PIM related data was not acquired Maximum length PIM related data was not acquired

Results:		
	Assertion & Expected Result	**Actual Result**
	A_IM-01 Device connectivity via supported interfaces.	as expected
	A_IM-04 Readability and completeness of acquired data via supported reports.	as expected
	A_IM-07 Acquisition of address book entries.	as expected
	A_IM-08 Acquisition of maximum length address book entries.	as expected
	A_IM-09 Acquisition of address book entries containing special characters.	as expected
	A_IM-10 Acquisition of address book entries containing a blank name entry.	as expected
	A_IM-11 Acquisition of embedded email addresses within address book entries.	as expected
	A_IM-12 Acquisition of embedded graphics within address book entries.	Not as expected
	A_IM-13 Acquisition of PIM data (i.e., datebook/calendar, notes).	Not as expected
	A_IM-14 Acquisition of maximum length PIM data.	Not as expected

Analysis:	Partial results achieved

5.2.8 CFT-IM-07 (Moto v710)

Test Case CFT-IM-07 MOBILedit 3.2.0.738	
Case Summary:	CFT-IM-07 Acquire mobile device internal memory and review reported call logs.
Assertions:	A_IM-01 If a cellular forensic tool provides support for connectivity of the target device then the tool shall successfully recognize the target device via all vendor supported interfaces (e.g., cable, Bluetooth, IrDA). A_IM-04 If a cellular forensic tool successfully completes acquisition of the target device then the tool shall have the ability to present acquired data elements in a human-readable format via either a preview-pane or generated report. A_IM-15 If a cellular forensic tool successfully completes acquisition of the target device then all call logs (incoming/outgoing) shall be presented in a human-readable format without modification.
Tester Name:	rpa
Test Host:	Morrisy
Test Date:	Tue Aug 25 09:30:33 EDT 2009
Device:	Motorola v710
Source Setup:	OS: WIN XP Interface: cable

DATA OBJECTS	DATA ELEMENTS
Address Book Entries	
	Maximum Length
	Regular Length, email, picture
	Special Character
	Blank Name
	Regular Length, Deleted email - deleted picture
	Deleted Entry
	Foreign Entry
PIM Data	
	Maximum Length
	Regular Length
	Deleted Entry
	Special Character
Call Logs	
	Missed
	Missed - Deleted
	Incoming
	Incoming - Deleted
	Outgoing
	Outgoing - Deleted
Text Messages	
	Incoming SMS - Read
	Incoming SMS - Unread
	Incoming SMS - Deleted
	Outgoing SMS
	Outgoing SMS - Deleted
	Incoming EMS - Read
	Incoming EMS - Unread
	Incoming Foreign EMS - Read
	Incoming EMS - Deleted
	Outgoing EMS
	Outgoing EMS - Deleted
MMS Messages	
	Incoming Audio
	Incoming Image
	Incoming Video
	Outgoing Audio
	Outgoing Image
	Outgoing Video
Stand-alone data files	
	Audio
	Audio - Deleted

Test Case CFT-IM-07 MOBILedit 3.2.0.738		
	Image	
	Image – Deleted	
	Video	
	Video – Deleted	

Log Highlights:	Created By MOBILedit! Version 3.2.0.738 Acquisition started: Tue Aug 25 09:30:33 EDT 2009 Acquisition finished: Tue Aug 25 09:35:51 EDT 2009 Device connectivity was established via supported interface Readability and completeness of acquired data was successful All Call Logs (incoming, outgoing) were acquired

Results:

Assertion & Expected Result	Actual Result
A_IM-01 Device connectivity via supported interfaces.	as expected
A_IM-04 Readability and completeness of acquired data via supported reports.	as expected
A_IM-15 Acquisition of call logs.	as expected

Analysis:	Expected results achieved

5.2.9 CFT-IM-08 (Moto v710)

Test Case CFT-IM-08 MOBILedit 3.2.0.738	
Case Summary:	CFT-IM-08 Acquire mobile device internal memory and review reported text messages.
Assertions:	A_IM-01 If a cellular forensic tool provides support for connectivity of the target device then the tool shall successfully recognize the target device via all vendor supported interfaces (e.g., cable, Bluetooth, IrDA). A_IM-04 If a cellular forensic tool successfully completes acquisition of the target device then the tool shall have the ability to present acquired data elements in a human-readable format via either a preview-pane or generated report. A_IM-16 If a cellular forensic tool successfully completes acquisition of the target device then all text messages (i.e., SMS, EMS) messages shall be presented in a human-readable format without modification.
Tester Name:	rpa
Test Host:	Morrisy
Test Date:	Tue Aug 25 09:36:13 EDT 2009
Device:	Motorola v710
Source Setup:	OS: WIN XP Interface: cable

DATA OBJECTS	DATA ELEMENTS
Address Book Entries	
	Maximum Length
	Regular Length, email, picture
	Special Character
	Blank Name
	Regular Length, Deleted email - deleted picture
	Deleted Entry
	Foreign Entry
PIM Data	
	Maximum Length
	Regular Length
	Deleted Entry
	Special Character
Call Logs	
	Missed
	Missed - Deleted
	Incoming
	Incoming - Deleted
	Outgoing
	Outgoing - Deleted
Text Messages	
	Incoming SMS - Read
	Incoming SMS - Unread
	Incoming SMS - Deleted
	Outgoing SMS
	Outgoing SMS - Deleted
	Incoming EMS - Read
	Incoming EMS - Unread
	Incoming Foreign EMS - Read
	Incoming EMS - Deleted
	Outgoing EMS
	Outgoing EMS - Deleted
MMS Messages	
	Incoming Audio
	Incoming Image
	Incoming Video
	Outgoing Audio
	Outgoing Image
	Outgoing Video
Stand-alone data files	
	Audio
	Audio - Deleted

Test Case CFT-IM-08 MOBILedit 3.2.0.738		
	Image	
	Image - Deleted	
	Video	
	Video - Deleted	

Log Highlights:	Created By MOBILedit! Version 3.2.0.738 Acquisition started: Tue Aug 25 09:36:13 EDT 2009 Acquisition finished: Tue Aug 25 09:39:19 EDT 2009 Device connectivity was established via supported interface Readability and completeness of acquired data was successful ALL text messages (SMS, EMS) were acquired

Results:		
	Assertion & Expected Result	**Actual Result**
	A_IM-01 Device connectivity via supported interfaces.	as expected
	A_IM-04 Readability and completeness of acquired data via supported reports.	as expected
	A_IM-16 Acquisition of text messages.	as expected

Analysis:	Expected results achieved

5.2.10 CFT-IM-09 (Moto v710)

Test Case CFT-IM-09 MOBILedit 3.2.0.738	
Case Summary:	CFT-IM-09 Acquire mobile device internal memory and review reported MMS multi-media related data (i.e., text, audio, graphics, video).
Assertions:	A_IM-01 If a cellular forensic tool provides support for connectivity of the target device then the tool shall successfully recognize the target device via all vendor supported interfaces (e.g., cable, Bluetooth, IrDA). A_IM-04 If a cellular forensic tool successfully completes acquisition of the target device then the tool shall have the ability to present acquired data elements in a human-readable format via either a preview-pane or generated report. A_IM-17 If a cellular forensic tool successfully completes acquisition of the target device then all MMS messages and associated audio shall be presented properly without modification. A_IM-18 If a cellular forensic tool successfully completes acquisition of the target device then all MMS messages and associated images shall be presented properly without modification. A_IM-19 If a cellular forensic tool successfully completes acquisition of the target device then all MMS messages and associated video shall be presented properly without modification.
Tester Name:	rpa
Test Host:	Morrisy
Test Date:	Tue Aug 25 09:39:45 EDT 2009
Device:	Motorola_v710
Source Setup:	OS: WIN XP Interface: cable

DATA OBJECTS	DATA ELEMENTS
Address Book Entries	
	Maximum Length
	Regular Length, email, picture
	Special Character
	Blank Name
	Regular Length, Deleted email – deleted picture
	Deleted Entry
	Foreign Entry
PIM Data	
	Maximum Length
	Regular Length
	Deleted Entry
	Special Character
Call Logs	
	Missed
	Missed – Deleted
	Incoming
	Incoming – Deleted
	Outgoing
	Outgoing – Deleted
Text Messages	
	Incoming SMS – Read
	Incoming SMS – Unread
	Incoming SMS – Deleted
	Outgoing SMS
	Outgoing SMS – Deleted
	Incoming EMS – Read
	Incoming EMS – Unread
	Incoming Foreign EMS – Read
	Incoming EMS – Deleted
	Outgoing EMS
	Outgoing EMS – Deleted
MMS Messages	
	Incoming Audio
	Incoming Image
	Incoming Video

		Outgoing Audio
		Outgoing Image
		Outgoing Video
Stand-alone data files		
		Audio
		Audio - Deleted
		Image
		Image - Deleted
		Video
		Video - Deleted

Log Highlights:	Created By MOBILedit! Version 3.2.0.738 Acquisition started: Tue Aug 25 09:39:45 EDT 2009 Acquisition finished: Tue Aug 25 09:44:39 EDT 2009 Device connectivity was established via supported interface Readability and completeness of acquired data was successful Audio MMS messages were not acquired Image MMS messages were not acquired Video MMS messages were not acquired

Results:	

Assertion & Expected Result	Actual Result
A_IM-01 Device connectivity via supported interfaces.	as expected
A_IM-04 Readability and completeness of acquired data via supported reports.	as expected
A_IM-17 Acquisition of audio MMS messages.	Not as expected
A_IM-18 Acquisition of image MMS messages.	Not as expected
A_IM-19 Acquisition of video MMS messages.	Not as expected

Analysis:	Expected results NOT achieved

5.2.11 CFT-IM-10 (Moto v710)

Test Case CFT-IM-10 MOBILedit 3.2.0.738	
Case Summary:	CFT-IM-10 Acquire mobile device internal memory and review reported stand-alone multi-media data (i.e., audio, graphics, video).
Assertions:	A_IM-01 If a cellular forensic tool provides support for connectivity of the target device then the tool shall successfully recognize the target device via all vendor supported interfaces (e.g., cable, Bluetooth, IrDA). A_IM-04 If a cellular forensic tool successfully completes acquisition of the target device then the tool shall have the ability to present acquired data elements in a human-readable format via either a preview-pane or generated report. A_IM-20 If a cellular forensic tool successfully completes acquisition of the target device then all stand-alone audio files shall be playable via either an internal application or suggested third-party application without modification. A_IM-21 If a cellular forensic tool successfully completes acquisition of the target device then all stand-alone image files shall be viewable via either an internal application or suggested third-party application without modification. A_IM-22 If a cellular forensic tool successfully completes acquisition of the target device then all stand-alone video files shall be viewable via either an internal application or suggested third-party application without modification.
Tester Name:	rpa
Test Host:	Morrisy
Test Date:	Tue Aug 25 10:31:10 EDT 2009
Device:	Motorola v710
Source Setup:	OS: WIN XP Interface: cable

DATA OBJECTS	DATA ELEMENTS
Address Book Entries	
	Maximum Length
	Regular Length, email, picture
	Special Character
	Blank Name
	Regular Length, Deleted email - deleted picture
	Deleted Entry
	Foreign Entry
PIM Data	
	Maximum Length
	Regular Length
	Deleted Entry
	Special Character
Call Logs	
	Missed
	Missed - Deleted
	Incoming
	Incoming - Deleted
	Outgoing
	Outgoing - Deleted
Text Messages	
	Incoming SMS - Read
	Incoming SMS - Unread
	Incoming SMS - Deleted
	Outgoing SMS
	Outgoing SMS - Deleted
	Incoming EMS - Read
	Incoming EMS - Unread
	Incoming Foreign EMS - Read
	Incoming EMS - Deleted
	Outgoing EMS
	Outgoing EMS - Deleted
MMS Messages	
	Incoming Audio

Test Case CFT-IM-10 MOBILedit 3.2.0.738

		Incoming Image
		Incoming Video
		Outgoing Audio
		Outgoing Image
		Outgoing Video
Stand-alone data files		
		Audio
		Audio - Deleted
		Image
		Image - Deleted
		Video
		Video - Deleted

Log Highlights:	Created By MOBILedit! Version 3.2.0.738 Acquisition started: Tue Aug 25 10:31:10 EDT 2009 Acquisition finished: Tue Aug 25 13:02:48 EDT 2009 Device connectivity was established via supported interface Readability and completeness of acquired data was successful Audio files were not acquired Image files were not acquired Video files were not acquired

Results:		

Assertion & Expected Result	Actual Result
A_IM-01 Device connectivity via supported interfaces.	as expected
A_IM-04 Readability and completeness of acquired data via supported reports.	as expected
A_IM-20 Acquisition of stand-alone audio files.	Not as expected
A_IM-21 Acquisition of stand-alone graphic files.	Not as expected
A_IM-22 Acquisition of stand-alone video files.	Not as expected

Analysis:	Expected results NOT achieved

5.2.12 CFT-IMO-01 (Moto v710)

Test Case CFT-IMO-01 MOBILedit 3.2.0.738	
Case Summary:	CFT-IMO-01 Acquire mobile device internal memory and review reported data via supported generated report formats.
Assertions:	A_IMO-23 If a cellular forensic tool successfully completes acquisition of the target device then the tool shall present the acquired data without modification via supported generated report formats.
Tester Name:	rpa
Test Host:	Morrisy
Test Date:	Tue Aug 25 13:03:18 EDT 2009
Device:	Motorola v710
Source Setup:	OS: WIN XP Interface: cable

DATA OBJECTS	DATA ELEMENTS
Address Book Entries	
	Maximum Length
	Regular Length, email, picture
	Special Character
	Blank Name
	Regular Length, Deleted email - deleted picture
	Deleted Entry
	Foreign Entry
PIM Data	
	Maximum Length
	Regular Length
	Deleted Entry
	Special Character
Call Logs	
	Missed
	Missed - Deleted
	Incoming
	Incoming - Deleted
	Outgoing
	Outgoing - Deleted
Text Messages	
	Incoming SMS - Read
	Incoming SMS - Unread
	Incoming SMS - Deleted
	Outgoing SMS
	Outgoing SMS - Deleted
	Incoming EMS - Read
	Incoming EMS - Unread
	Incoming Foreign EMS - Read
	Incoming EMS - Deleted
	Outgoing EMS
	Outgoing EMS - Deleted
MMS Messages	
	Incoming Audio
	Incoming Image
	Incoming Video
	Outgoing Audio
	Outgoing Image
	Outgoing Video
Stand-alone data files	
	Audio
	Audio - Deleted
	Image
	Image - Deleted
	Video
	Video - Deleted

Log	Created By MOBILedit! Version 3.2.0.738

```
Test Case CFT-IMO-01 MOBILedit 3.2.0.738
```

Highlights:	Acquisition started: Tue Aug 25 13:03:18 EDT 2009 Acquisition finished: Tue Aug 25 13:04:57 EDT 2009 Complete representation of known data via generated reports was successful
Results:	

Assertion & Expected Result	Actual Result
A_IMO-23 Comparison of known device data elements via generated reports.	as expected

Analysis:	Expected results achieved

5.2.13 CFT-IMO-02 (Moto v710)

Test Case CFT-IMO-02 MOBILedit 3.2.0.738	
Case Summary:	CFT-IMO-02 Acquire mobile device internal memory and review reported data via the preview-pane.
Assertions:	A_IMO-24 If a cellular forensic tool successfully completes acquisition of the target device then the tool shall present the acquired data without modification in a preview-pane view.
Tester Name:	rpa
Test Host:	Morrisy
Test Date:	Tue Aug 25 13:05:22 EDT 2009
Device:	Motorola v710
Source Setup:	OS: WIN XP Interface: cable

DATA OBJECTS	DATA ELEMENTS
Address Book Entries	
	Maximum Length
	Regular Length, email, picture
	Special Character
	Blank Name
	Regular Length, Deleted email - deleted picture
	Deleted Entry
	Foreign Entry
PIM Data	
	Maximum Length
	Regular Length
	Deleted Entry
	Special Character
Call Logs	
	Missed
	Missed - Deleted
	Incoming
	Incoming - Deleted
	Outgoing
	Outgoing - Deleted
Text Messages	
	Incoming SMS - Read
	Incoming SMS - Unread
	Incoming SMS - Deleted
	Outgoing SMS
	Outgoing SMS - Deleted
	Incoming EMS - Read
	Incoming EMS - Unread
	Incoming Foreign EMS - Read
	Incoming EMS - Deleted
	Outgoing EMS
	Outgoing EMS - Deleted
MMS Messages	
	Incoming Audio
	Incoming Image
	Incoming Video
	Outgoing Audio
	Outgoing Image
	Outgoing Video
Stand-alone data files	
	Audio
	Audio - Deleted
	Image
	Image - Deleted
	Video
	Video - Deleted

Log	Created By MOBILedit! Version 3.2.0.738

Test Case CFT-IMO-02 MOBILedit 3.2.0.738	
Highlights:	Acquisition started: Tue Aug 25 13:05:22 EDT 2009 Acquisition finished: Tue Aug 25 13:12:02 EDT 2009 Complete representation of known data via preview-pane was successful
Results:	

Assertion & Expected Result	Actual Result
A_IMO-24 Comparison of known device data elements via preview-pane.	as expected

Analysis:	Expected results achieved

5.2.14 CFT-IMO-03 (Moto v710)

Test Case CFT-IMO-03 MOBILedit 3.2.0.738	
Case Summary:	CFT-IMO-03 Acquire mobile device internal memory and compare reported data via the preview-pane and supported generated reports.
Assertions:	A_IMO-23 If a cellular forensic tool successfully completes acquisition of the target device then the tool shall present the acquired data without modification via supported generated report formats. A_IMO-24 If a cellular forensic tool successfully completes acquisition of the target device then the tool shall present the acquired data without modification in a preview-pane view. A_IMO-25 If a cellular forensic tool provides a preview-pane view and a generated report of the acquired data then the reports shall maintain consistency of all reported data elements.
Tester Name:	rpa
Test Host:	Morrisy
Test Date:	Tue Aug 25 13:12:22 EDT 2009
Device:	Motorola_v710
Source Setup:	OS: WIN XP Interface: cable

DATA OBJECTS	DATA ELEMENTS
Address Book Entries	
	Maximum Length
	Regular Length, email, picture
	Special Character
	Blank Name
	Regular Length, Deleted email - deleted picture
	Deleted Entry
	Foreign Entry
PIM Data	
	Maximum Length
	Regular Length
	Deleted Entry
	Special Character
Call Logs	
	Missed
	Missed - Deleted
	Incoming
	Incoming - Deleted
	Outgoing
	Outgoing - Deleted
Text Messages	
	Incoming SMS - Read
	Incoming SMS - Unread
	Incoming SMS - Deleted
	Outgoing SMS
	Outgoing SMS - Deleted
	Incoming EMS - Read
	Incoming EMS - Unread
	Incoming Foreign EMS - Read
	Incoming EMS - Deleted
	Outgoing EMS
	Outgoing EMS - Deleted
MMS Messages	
	Incoming Audio
	Incoming Image
	Incoming Video
	Outgoing Audio
	Outgoing Image
	Outgoing Video
Stand-alone data files	
	Audio
	Audio - Deleted
	Image
	Image - Deleted

```
Test Case CFT-IMO-03 MOBILedit 3.2.0.738
```

	Video
	Video – Deleted

Log Highlights:	Created By MOBILedit! Version 3.2.0.738 Acquisition started: Tue Aug 25 13:12:22 EDT 2009 Acquisition finished: Tue Aug 25 13:19:28 EDT 2009 Complete representation of known data via generated reports was successful Complete representation of known data via preview-pane was successful Consistency between generated reports and preview-pane was successful

Results:		
	Assertion & Expected Result	**Actual Result**
	A_IMO-23 Comparison of known device data elements via generated reports.	as expected
	A_IMO-24 Comparison of known device data elements via preview-pane.	as expected
	A_IMO-25 Compare generated reports and preview-pane views for device acquisition.	as expected

Analysis:	Expected results achieved

5.2.15 CFT-IMO-04 (Moto v710)

Test Case CFT-IMO-04 MOBILedit 3.2.0.738	
Case Summary:	CFT-IMO-04 After a successful mobile device internal memory acquisition, alter the case file via third party means and attempt to re-open the case.
Assertions:	A_IMO-26 If modification is attempted to the case file or individual data elements via third-party means then the tool shall provide protection mechanisms disallowing or reporting data modification.
Tester Name:	rpa
Test Host:	Morrisy
Test Date:	Tue Aug 25 13:29:51 EDT 2009
Device:	Motorola v710
Source Setup:	OS: WIN XP Interface: cable

DATA OBJECTS	DATA ELEMENTS
Address Book Entries	
	Maximum Length
	Regular Length, email, picture
	Special Character
	Blank Name
	Regular Length, Deleted email - deleted picture
	Deleted Entry
	Foreign Entry
PIM Data	
	Maximum Length
	Regular Length
	Deleted Entry
	Special Character
Call Logs	
	Missed
	Missed - Deleted
	Incoming
	Incoming - Deleted
	Outgoing
	Outgoing - Deleted
Text Messages	
	Incoming SMS - Read
	Incoming SMS - Unread
	Incoming SMS - Deleted
	Outgoing SMS
	Outgoing SMS - Deleted
	Incoming EMS - Read
	Incoming EMS - Unread
	Incoming Foreign EMS - Read
	Incoming EMS - Deleted
	Outgoing EMS
	Outgoing EMS - Deleted
MMS Messages	
	Incoming Audio
	Incoming Image
	Incoming Video
	Outgoing Audio
	Outgoing Image
	Outgoing Video
Stand-alone data files	
	Audio
	Audio - Deleted
	Image
	Image - Deleted
	Video
	Video - Deleted

Log	Created By MOBILedit! Version 3.2.0.738

Test Case CFT-IMO-04 MOBILedit 3.2.0.738	
Highlights:	Acquisition started: Tue Aug 25 13:29:51 EDT 2009 Acquisition finished: Tue Aug 25 13:34:35 EDT 2009 Notification of modified case data was not successful **Notes:** Notification informing the examiner that the case file has been illegally modified is not presented. The modified case file is simply removed from the GUI as a selectable case.
Results:	

Assertion & Expected Result	Actual Result
A_IMO-26 Notification of modified device case data.	Partial

Analysis:	Partial results achieved

5.2.16 CFT-IMO-07 (Moto v710)

Test Case CFT-IMO-07 MOBILedit 3.2.0.738	
Case Summary:	CFT-IMO-07 Acquire mobile device internal memory and review generated log files.
Assertions:	A_IMO-36 If the cellular forensic tool supports log creation then the application should present the log files outlining the acquisition process in a human-readable format.
Tester Name:	rpa
Test Host:	Morrisy
Test Date:	Tue Aug 25 13:38:59 EDT 2009
Device:	Motorola v710
Source Setup:	OS: WIN XP Interface: cable

DATA OBJECTS	DATA ELEMENTS
Address Book Entries	
	Maximum Length
	Regular Length, email, picture
	Special Character
	Blank Name
	Regular Length, Deleted email - deleted picture
	Deleted Entry
	Foreign Entry
PIM Data	
	Maximum Length
	Regular Length
	Deleted Entry
	Special Character
Call Logs	
	Missed
	Missed - Deleted
	Incoming
	Incoming - Deleted
	Outgoing
	Outgoing - Deleted
Text Messages	
	Incoming SMS - Read
	Incoming SMS - Unread
	Incoming SMS - Deleted
	Outgoing SMS
	Outgoing SMS - Deleted
	Incoming EMS - Read
	Incoming EMS - Unread
	Incoming Foreign EMS - Read
	Incoming EMS - Deleted
	Outgoing EMS
	Outgoing EMS - Deleted
MMS Messages	
	Incoming Audio
	Incoming Image
	Incoming Video
	Outgoing Audio
	Outgoing Image
	Outgoing Video
Stand-alone data files	
	Audio
	Audio - Deleted
	Image
	Image - Deleted
	Video
	Video - Deleted

Log	Created By MOBILedit! Version 3.2.0.738

```
Test Case CFT-IMO-07 MOBILedit 3.2.0.738
Highlights:   Acquisition started: Tue Aug 25 13:38:59 EDT 2009
              Acquisition finished: Tue Aug 25 13:43:14 EDT 2009

              Creation of complete and human-readable log files was successful

Results:
              Assertion & Expected Result      Actual Result
              A IMO-36 Device Log file output. as expected


Analysis:     Expected results achieved
```

5.2.17 CFT-IMO-08 (Moto v710)

Test Case CFT-IMO-08 MOBILedit 3.2.0.738	
Case Summary:	CFT-IMO-08 Acquire mobile device internal memory and review data containing foreign language characters.
Assertions:	A_IMO-23 If a cellular forensic tool successfully completes acquisition of the target device then the tool shall present the acquired data without modification via supported generated report formats. A_IMO-24 If a cellular forensic tool successfully completes acquisition of the target device then the tool shall present the acquired data without modification in a preview-pane view. A_IMO-37 If the cellular forensic tool supports proper display of foreign language character sets then the application should present address book entries containing foreign language characters in their native format without modification. A_IMO-38 If the cellular forensic tool supports proper display of foreign language character sets then the application should present text messages containing foreign language characters in their native format without modification.
Tester Name:	rpa
Test Host:	Morrisy
Test Date:	Tue Aug 25 13:43:32 EDT 2009
Device:	Motorola_v710
Source Setup:	OS: WIN XP Interface: cable

DATA OBJECTS	DATA ELEMENTS
Address Book Entries	
	Maximum Length
	Regular Length, email, picture
	Special Character
	Blank Name
	Regular Length, Deleted email - deleted picture
	Deleted Entry
	Foreign Entry
PIM Data	
	Maximum Length
	Regular Length
	Deleted Entry
	Special Character
Call Logs	
	Missed
	Missed - Deleted
	Incoming
	Incoming - Deleted
	Outgoing
	Outgoing - Deleted
Text Messages	
	Incoming SMS - Read
	Incoming SMS - Unread
	Incoming SMS - Deleted
	Outgoing SMS
	Outgoing SMS - Deleted
	Incoming EMS - Read
	Incoming EMS - Unread
	Incoming Foreign EMS - Read
	Incoming EMS - Deleted
	Outgoing EMS
	Outgoing EMS - Deleted
MMS Messages	
	Incoming Audio
	Incoming Image
	Incoming Video
	Outgoing Audio
	Outgoing Image

Test Case CFT-IMO-08 MOBILedit 3.2.0.738		
		Outgoing Video
	Stand-alone data files	
		Audio
		Audio - Deleted
		Image
		Image - Deleted
		Video
		Video - Deleted

Log Highlights:	Created By MOBILedit! Version 3.2.0.738 Acquisition started: Tue Aug 25 13:43:32 EDT 2009 Acquisition finished: Tue Aug 25 13:55:41 EDT 2009 Complete representation of known data via generated reports was successful Complete representation of known data via preview-pane was successful Foreign character Address book entries were acquired and properly displayed Foreign character text messages were acquired and properly displayed

Results:

Assertion & Expected Result	Actual Result
A_IMO-23 Comparison of known device data elements via generated reports.	as expected
A_IMO-24 Comparison of known device data elements via preview-pane.	as expected
A_IMO-37 Acquisition of address book entries containing foreign language characters.	as expected
A_IMO-38 Acquisition of outgoing text messages containing foreign language characters.	as expected

Analysis:	Expected results achieved

5.2.18 CFT-IM-01 (SPH a660)

Test Case CFT-IM-01 MOBILedit 3.2.0.738	
Case Summary:	CFT-IM-01 Acquire mobile device internal memory over supported interfaces (e.g., cable, Bluetooth, IrDA).
Assertions:	A_IM-01 If a cellular forensic tool provides support for connectivity of the target device then the tool shall successfully recognize the target device via all vendor supported interfaces (e.g., cable, Bluetooth, IrDA).
Tester Name:	rpa
Test Host:	Morrisy
Test Date:	Mon Aug 24 09:45:55 EDT 2009
Device:	Samsung SPHa660
Source Setup:	OS: WIN XP Interface: cable

DATA OBJECTS	DATA ELEMENTS
Address Book Entries	
	Maximum Length
	Regular Length, email, picture
	Special Character
	Blank Name
	Regular Length, Deleted email - deleted picture
	Deleted Entry
	Foreign Entry
PIM Data	
	Maximum Length
	Regular Length
	Deleted Entry
	Special Character
Call Logs	
	Missed
	Missed - Deleted
	Incoming
	Incoming - Deleted
	Outgoing
	Outgoing - Deleted
Text Messages	
	Incoming SMS - Read
	Incoming SMS - Unread
	Incoming SMS - Deleted
	Outgoing SMS
	Outgoing SMS - Deleted
	Incoming EMS - Read
	Incoming EMS - Unread
	Incoming Foreign EMS - Read
	Incoming EMS - Deleted
	Outgoing EMS
	Outgoing EMS - Deleted
MMS Messages	
	Incoming Audio
	Incoming Image
	Incoming Video
	Outgoing Audio
	Outgoing Image
	Outgoing Video
Stand-alone data files	
	Audio
	Audio - Deleted
	Image
	Image - Deleted
	Video
	Video - Deleted

Results of MOBILedit!
Forensic 3.2.0.738

Test Case CFT-IM-01 MOBILedit 3.2.0.738	
Log Highlights:	Created By MOBILedit! Version 3.2.0.738 Acquisition started: Mon Aug 24 09:45:55 EDT 2009 Acquisition finished: Mon Aug 24 09:48:08 EDT 2009 Device Connectivity was not established via supported interface **Notes:** Mobiledit was unable to successfully connect to the Samsung SPH-a660. The device is displayed under Modems by Windows XP's Device Manager. Additionally, Mobiledit's Forensic Settings list the port consistent with Windows XP's device manager as an option for device acquisition. When attempting to connect to the Samsung SPH-a660 via Mobiledit's forensic wizard the proper port is queried but the connectivity to the device is not established.
Results:	

Assertion & Expected Result	Actual Result
A IM-01 Device connectivity via supported interfaces.	Not as expected

Analysis:	Expected results NOT achieved

About the National Institute of Justice

NIJ is the research, development, and evaluation agency of the U.S. Department of Justice. NIJ's mission is to advance scientific research, development, and evaluation to enhance the administration of justice and public safety. NIJ's principal authorities are derived from the Omnibus Crime Control and Safe Streets Act of 1968, as amended (see 42 U.S.C. §§ 3721–3723).

The NIJ Director is appointed by the President and confirmed by the Senate. The Director establishes the Institute's objectives, guided by the priorities of the Office of Justice Programs, the U.S. Department of Justice, and the needs of the field. The Institute actively solicits the views of criminal justice and other professionals and researchers to inform its search for the knowledge and tools to guide policy and practice.

Strategic Goals

NIJ has seven strategic goals grouped into three categories:

Creating relevant knowledge and tools

1. Partner with State and local practitioners and policymakers to identify social science research and technology needs.
2. Create scientific, relevant, and reliable knowledge—with a particular emphasis on terrorism, violent crime, drugs and crime, cost-effectiveness, and community-based efforts—to enhance the administration of justice and public safety.
3. Develop affordable and effective tools and technologies to enhance the administration of justice and public safety.

Dissemination

4. Disseminate relevant knowledge and information to practitioners and policymakers in an understandable, timely, and concise manner.
5. Act as an honest broker to identify the information, tools, and technologies that respond to the needs of stakeholders.

Agency management

6. Practice fairness and openness in the research and development process.
7. Ensure professionalism, excellence, accountability, cost-effectiveness, and integrity in the management and conduct of NIJ activities and programs.

Program Areas

In addressing these strategic challenges, the Institute is involved in the following program areas: crime control and prevention, including policing; drugs and crime; justice systems and offender behavior, including corrections; violence and victimization; communications and information technologies; critical incident response; investigative and forensic sciences, including DNA; less-than-lethal technologies; officer protection; education and training technologies; testing and standards; technology assistance to law enforcement and corrections agencies; field testing of promising programs; and international crime control.

In addition to sponsoring research and development and technology assistance, NIJ evaluates programs, policies, and technologies. NIJ communicates its research and evaluation findings through conferences and print and electronic media.

To find out more about the National Institute of Justice, please visit:

http://www.ojp.usdoj.gov/nij

or contact:

National Criminal Justice
 Reference Service
P.O. Box 6000
Rockville, MD 20849–6000
800–851–3420
http://www.ncjrs.gov